DOG WHISTLE POLITICS

New & Selected Poems by
Michael Paul

—LUMMOX Press—

ISBN: 978-1-929878-94-9

Published by Lummox Press
PO Box 5301
San Pedro, CA 90733

www.lummoxpress.com

Printed in the United States of America

Acknowledgements:

Grateful acknowledgement is given to the publishers. Some of these poems, or versions of them, have appeared in the following publications: Blue Satellite, Spillway, Pearl, Dufus, FTS, 2:00 P.M. Thursday, The Valley Contemporary Poets Anthologies, The Daily Word, Incidental Buildings & Accidental Beauty; and in the chapbooks: Radio Cats, Collage, Wanderer from The Inevitable Press; American Hieroglyph, and The Turning Point from FarStarFire Press; and Bird Interpretations from Cassowary Press.

Esse Quam Videre

State motto of North Carolina

O wizard of changes, teach me the lesson of flowing

Line from "the Water Song" by the Incredible String Band

It's time to quit polishing…and just *shine!*

from a conversation with Gary Parrish

Table of Contents

Introduction
The Portrait of the Artist as an Earthworm Divinator

As I WRITE THIS, THE SOUTHLAND HAS BEEN gullywashed by nearly three weeks of chilly rain storms. As the macadam pulls moisture back through networks of varicose cracks into the soil bed, we venture out for our bagged newspapers and try to avoid stepping on the drowned ooey-gooeys. A sorry obstacle course, that's what most of us would see.

Michael Paul (a highly talented artist with pen and pencil, now living well north of us) would step onto the driveway for his daily news and see a Flanders Field of ideas that tried to make it to higher ground. After reading the funny papers, he might try to draw a pen and ink landscape of what he saw. He would detail the annular segments in various stages of drying. He would capture the mating bands stilled in pools of water. Certainly, he would make it possible for us to see how the many pores on the earthworms' sides gasped a final time for air when they found themselves on compacted, rocky, or unyielding terrain. He would show us how they died, then he would show us how they dried. And then, with his poetry, he would show us how to read their meaning.

Everything Michael places on his canvas or in a poem—line, color, the picture plane itself—shudders, sways, and wriggles with meaning, but he imposes no external meaning on anything he depicts. There are no cheap tricks with shadows or frequencies of colored dots or hidden breasts in the fading tulips. His eyes and ears are organs of such accuracy and certainty that he draws meaning out of its textual hiding places and allows it to stand alone, fully revealed and uneditorialized. He would accurately use the word *stranded* to describe the worms' condition, because that is what a naturalist of his decades of experience prowling Southern California's mountains and scrubland would say. And yet, because he is also a poet of exceptional sensibilities, he would also know that *stranded* conveys a wealth of emotional states that earthworms cannot express, dogs might not be able to hear, and the human heart struggles to pinpoint.

Michael will introduce you to a host of people he loves in *Dog Whistle Politics*—his wife, his daughters, his neighbors from Cerritos, a girl you may already know who just wants a pick-up truck, his parents, and Yahweh Himself. Though he will present them in dream states, in periods of passage, and materializing from surrealist buses, he will depict them with his naturalist's accuracy. He will show you that people, like earthworms, can become stranded when they attempt to mate or move to higher elevations. He will show you that people, like earthworms, can move the world—a place he calls "a ball that chance built."

Without trying to tell you a thing, he will show you everything.

Amélie Frank
January 7, 2011

DOG WHISTLE
POLITICS

Dog Whistle Politics

Ladies and Gentlemen our presentation
will begin promptly at the equinox
or solar eclipse,
whichever occurs first. Meanwhile,
our lovely attendants shall attempt to guess
your exact atomic weight.

Place your wagers, and remember, it's all for charity.

We are, it should come as no surprise, permeable
membranes, permitting entrance if presented
hospital flowers, semi-wilted, in a rusted
George Washington plug tobacco tin.

That last bouquet was useless, got no one absolutely no where.

We request your quiet attention; this is
after all a one-way valve, (unless we specify otherwise),
only having traffic with:
criminals,
madmen,
little children,
loose women,
spiritual types of all stripes,

arty-farty boho folks, and faithless dogs
named Freedom.

At our intermission we shall be serving complimentary hors d'oeuvres—

turpentine cocktails,
grist for the mill,
free lunches,
amnesia,
finger sandwiches
(made from actual fingers!),
and a quaint little pasta
with a piquant sauce
concocted
from your deepest fears.

The Catalog of Unwritten Poems

A cellar full of wine
bottles, sleeping on their sides,
heads down, dreaming
drunkards' dreams.

A rhetorical question,
in a Yiddish accent, George Jessell
(with a lazy eyelid) asking:
"who is like god?"

The attempt to write
upon the inside surface
of a wedding band,
purchased for "the other woman,"
by another man.

The epistemology
of insects, and brown-skinned
fancy-dancers,
chanting.

The portrait of the artist
as a young automobile accident.

An attempt to decipher
the acid vision hieroglyphics
of acoustical ceilings.

The endorphin junkie's lament.

The moral imperative
of extensive tattooing.

The portrait of the artist
as a middle-aged credenza.

A secret history
of the victories
of small potatoes.

The learned distrust
of anyone named Howard.

Epiphanies in pop songs—
life changing illuminations
in box-office flops.

The portrait of the artist
as a Dead Letter File.

Sidereal time in a bottle,
(from the cellar in the first stanza),
decanting streams of data.

The elegant flare
of a young girl's hips,
drawn with deft lines
on the insides
of your eyelids.

The death of love, displayed in toto
from Chain-Stoke to rigor mortis,
and finally its ghosts arrival
on your doorstep,
carrying
a toothbrush.

Oneironauts

In my sister's dream redemption comes
in the form of a pick-up truck.
In mine, my father, dead for decades,

drives a yellow bus to the shore
where bilingual fish explain
all secret knowledge.

In mother's dream Christ appeared to her
after the manner of Yahweh disclosing
his backside to Moses,

but it didn't involve vehicles—
just a tree, a red flannel shirt,
and dungarees. Cars are omens

in my wife's dreams; their portent
depending upon make, model, mileage,
Kelly Blue Book value, but above all—

who is behind the wheel of this latest model
augury? Who drives my sister's pick-up
while she pulls the walking wounded

over the tailgate into safety?
And who could possibly imagine my surprise
when the folding door hissed open

in my dream, and the driver of the bus
was my dad, finally come to take me
to the place where the real answers are.

The Americanization of Ooga-Booga

Borders blur—expand and contract
like breathing—
in this cartography of the heart.

We lived on borrowed time,
in close proximity to danger
and salvation, when we
were young, when you

became for me the litmus
of bigotry—the evidence
of difference.

I became a cub scout at seven,
I will never forget that small
first loss of innocence, by the water
fountain, when Tom Jones asked
if there were "colors" in my den.

Oblivious, I asked him what he meant,
so he pointed at you,
and my colorblindness was cured.

Winston Spratt, no relation to Jack,
brother to Junebug—I wonder
what's become of you, as I recall
that last bittersweet trip
down the boulevard, blasting
a cigar-sized spliff and singing:

batcha boola bonke
oman selele banse bavo
zhe a vo, wogalala banse bavo

Our bicycles, our boyhood, were ancient history.
Now you were at the wheel
of a lowered Chevy, driving us
down the streets that defined us—
divided us forever.

Asa Nisi Masa

I am thinking of a word, a shibboleth
scribbled in Cherokee, which signifies
a place where we might meet
unless you accidentally mispronounce it
as percussion and ocean sounds.

It is rather like the child's word,
the magical word, the one the mentalist
divined from Mastroianni's mind in 8½.

Remember?

Dear reader if you do, you are either
well versed in Italian cinema, or
coming up hard on senior citizen discounts.

I will give you a hint:

I recall a beat-up VW, squealing around the schoolyard,
an older couple, disguised with wax lips
and Buddy Holly glasses with fake noses;
shooting water pistols at us and laughing
their asses off. I took them as my paradigm
of maturity.

Does that help?

I fear, unless someone from the Paint Clan comes
to whisper something in your ear, we may never meet.

Do you have my word yet?
Do you have your own?

Directions to the Next World

for Brendan Constantine

Follow the crows who've finished
the day shift, flying north-west.

The crows follow women in severe suits,
their chorus of stilettos. In the trees

the chirping of the smaller birds
sounds exactly like adding machines.

The women follow repentant gunmen,
who, taking parables very literally,

amputate their trigger fingers.
Follow the itch in their phantom digits

pointing toward the bodhisattva
with his back to you, by a tree;

keeper of the X-Ray mandala,
the map to the next world.

Approach slowly and press your question
against him, until your dark question

turns as white as an insistent thumb
jammed upon the doorbell of heaven

Dear Doctor
to Matthew Mars

Forgive these
erasure marks. False steps and feints
toward speaking something into existence. Like

small worlds flung from lips and fingertips,
some crude and inchoate as moons, others
fearfully and wonderfully
given over to tourism.

One speaks of invisible engines,
another of secret rooms;
then of course we have the synthesis
of hyacinths and biscuits.

This could be a conversation
if we communicated telepathically
and our bodies forgotten languages
suddenly returned. Here's a clue:

your name is the abbreviation
of a mountain. Mine,
        the eponym of an archangel,
        the chief apostle, and
        a certain person
tenderly disposed toward
the drunk and disorderly.

Yours is the Art & Science
of the Doo-Wah-Diddy, decryptions
from your skin. Mine
is just to keep the brush and thud—
whitenoise to mask my tinnitus.

I am alone now with the ringing in my ears, and

Doctor, you were never dear
to me, just a useful, albeit charming,
means to an end, until now, sir.

Thank you for singing at my wedding.

He, being dead, yet speaks, pipes, writes

Listen:
lessons in bone.

Jazzman lifts brass, like knife,
riffing filigrees of sadness, sonic scrimshaw
upon hammers, anvils, stirrups, all
the smallest ossicles of this
benighted head.
Bowed head. Eyes burn.

Listen:
my love comes,
kittenlike,
bearing gifts. Four roses odorless
and still as newly killed mice;
lays them out, like my heart,
at her feet,
with the news of her leaving.

Alone now with the jazzman,
taking all the wine dark lines
of haunted face,
written by the blind luck draw
of double helix,
scribed by horn

(not ax, but knife)
now sharpened on the castanet clatter
of my love's knocking,
my love's leaving. I raise

a toast:
a cup of gladness
turned to vinegar and gall.
Put four roses into it:

The color of memory.
The complexion of time.
The shade of solitude.
The hue and pattern of
the chiaroscuro coloratura
the jazzman scratches on my bones.

Listen: I will
raise a toast to the woman,
whose tuition, though bitter,
costly as a mouthful of ants,
is the unwilling dues
I pay to hear
all the way to my bones,
that hard bought beauty
of the blues.

Smoke & Mirrors

The cigarettes weep,
alone in the dark on a narrow bed.
After twenty-four years
they are finally divorced.

All they want,
all they can think about,
is the way it used to be. How you would turn
to them to be the punctuation

for all the finished moments
of your days. Interrogative. Exclamation point.

Period.

How you gave them your lips,
your caresses, as they burned
and filled you,

taking your shape.

Graffito

And so we drive through weather & night
outlining the coast with our lights
in an evanescent calligraphy, like

an ideogram for the two of us,
and the suchness of earth & water.

Graceful, dramatic, frightening
as the breathtaking dive the continent takes
into the misnamed sea.

Everything about this moment
from the tire hiss to the intermittent
metronome of the wipers,
delineates a character, much like

the stylish gang-write I saw, on the black
metal backdrop of a streetlight in Santa Cruz;
the one which made me wonder
if archeologists of the future would find it elegant, but indecipherable.

The jitterbug line of light we describe
along the ragged edge of our world
becomes our secret art & text—

its translation known
only to us.

Of Hair

for Amélie Frank

My eyebrows are islands
in a corrugated sea
of skin, the last outposts
of the dark hair of my youth.

A kind of Tir-na-n-og
on the boney promontory
of my brow.

Everywhere else, all the furred continents,
islands, atolls, and archipelagoes of my body
are turning to salt.

Even in the musky nether regions
of the south, little pale messengers
of mortality are popping up.

When I asked my Sister why this is so,
she told me that the brows and lashes
are a coarser, hardier breed

of hair, and
always the last to go.

This explains
why, on the milk-white planet
of my Sister's body,
the only follicular survivors
of the chemotherapeutic holocaust
are her brows and lashes,

the last outposts of what St. Paul called
a woman's glory

flying proud, like tiny flags

of life.

Poem reverse engineered from an assemblage which began life as a kitchen drawer in a shack on Signal Hill

There is no mezzuzah on our doorpost,
only this brownish collection of relics,
mementos mori:

pine cone, rock, exploded clock,
a letter from a lover, another
from a faithless friend.

Each thing compartmented
as the artist's heart, and sharing
the phylactery's conceit:

the quantification of the invisible.

Nacre from the shores of the North;
driftwood, and Dr. Rumney's
mentholyptus snuff. In pictures

within pictures, an Indian in his own frame
stares away, while a renaissance maiden
ponders detritus as revisionist history.

Beneath the maid there's a brass box lid

from India. Above her, an earring's echo
in a shell from the beach at San Miguel.

A lifetime written in a shadow box.

Selenite from Arkansas, the five-
fingered leaf from Muir Woods, the symmetry
of a seed pod from our honeymoon walk

One unbroken wish
bone from our first Thanksgiving. Perhaps the glory
of art outlasting the little tempest of our lives

is written in the prophet's song—we pick
and choose among this rubble like bricoleurs-
selecting this and scrapping that, to somehow render

beauty for ashes, the oil of joy for mourning.

Santa Ana Canyon Suite

for Sarah Maclay

At the edge of the mountains
we sit very still,
scratch ourselves raw
watching the moon move
through blood-colored leaves.

Close by, a house is burning.

Call it a busy country
road (which is what it is)
this damnation in faint praise
this arterial obstruction.

Father used to hear his blood
susurrating through his veins. At night
we can hear the whirr of the economy
from our balcony
here
at Exile Hotel.

Electra brings us hibiscus
    and mimosa
        in the morning.

Later, languid Asian boys with slow smiles

and heavy-lidded eyes
will pamper us
here at the terminus
of the millennium
of the continent
of our unhappiness.

My lover gives me cayenne
and honey, in apple
cider vinegar,
as an anodyne.

The arbiters of sanity
gave her mineral salts
and labels, when she wept
and weeded someone else's garden.

So while
the architects of neglect
construct themselves into corners
with piles of books, and insist
on civility,

we wash down crow
with wine, here in our funny
microclimate,
and wait for healing.

Five Haiku

Dolores River

> White noise through soft pines,
> half moon over dark river,
> rain laughs on our tent.

Mesa Verde

> Salt lick, after hike,
> hollow of your collar-bone;
> suddenly—a deer!

Cougar Crest

> Burnt trees shed black skin,
> white flowers sway, bow low to
> hymns of urgent bees.

Whiting Ranch

>Sandstone and soft place,
>apple bread cheese wine and kiss;
>shy the reaching trees.

Chaco Canyon

>My eyes swallow you,
>watching water sing down stones,
>the curve of your leg

Riddle

An ox pulls a house behind,
A boomerang before the door.

Behind the door a man rejoices,
Epsilon by name.

Epsilon rejoices before
The hook—Waw—Digamma.

Another boomerang (!) this one
The symbol of gravity.

Behind gravity there is a rope,
And then a hand,

And then another hand,
Dotted and tailed, the last to join the procession.

A hill slope, and then
A Semite passing into Greece,

Taking the shape of the suture connecting
The occipital and parietal bones of the skull.

Water precedes fish.
Tiny Omicron comes before the mouth.

A monkey in front of a head.
A tooth before a mark.

A hook, and another, and then another,
(Epsilon still rejoicing behind the door)

Followed by Samekh, also know as Chi;
And his partners:

Upsilon the Penultimate
Always going before Zed—

Passing out of Egypt into Palestine,
From glyph to rune and on into Rome...

What are we?

Small Diorama

All the skeletons
In my closet
Fashion skins
From my old drum heads

They cant and caterwaul
Chant and chuff

Succubae and automata
With a life of their own

Study them, and they dissolve
Into
       Pixels
             Rasters
                  Phosphenes

Binary smoke signals
Synaptic rabbit trails
Electro-chemical cocktails with dangerous side effects

Narcotic music

Unable to unmake them
I must accommodate their movements, my house

Is crowded with odors, notions
Attars and reveries
Infidelities and apostasies

The spunk smell of carob trees
The stolen apple sweetness
Of that first illicit kiss

One numb orgasm in another man's mouth

These are my specters
Violating peace treaties
Like Indians leaving reservations

The places of broken dreams

Trio
(a found poem)

1.

He wrote
Of childhoods
Fair and apprehensive
Morning.
Of earthly appetites,
Of metaphysical glimmerings.
The cocksure boundlessness
Of young married life;
The erosion of all these things
And the autumnal color,
The fall and wind drift
Of our certainties.

2.

His flamingo stands—
And disintegrates—
As a wholly original
Symbol, a pop culture
Monument to American ambition,
Illusionism, and giddily

Tasteless architecture;
A grandiose icon inhabited
By a motley crew
Of vernacular archetypes:
Mom,
Pop,
Multi-culti kids,
A wise old black man
And a blonde beach babe.

3.

He chooses maze design,
Because to him the maze
Suggests loss.
A desire to lose himself,
Or, more regressively, a desire
To cradle his consciousness
In a nest of softness,

Safety.

This Has Always Been Called the Valley of Smokes

Coming back to the queen we sense
first—
the manic energy.
Then—
we see brakelights blossom, and the sky
turn the color of rust.

We know we are home
when
we reach the pueblo
where none of the Indians speak to each other.
When
we reach the hive
where all the bees are solitary.

My woman is chanting
in the manner of a throat singer.

I keep telling her it isn't so bad, this isn't so bad,
while her fingers nervously fiddle
with the squelch knob,

trying to keep down the voices.

Another place is calling us
she says;
another place is calling out
and she can hear it
through the soles of her feet.

Camera Obscura

After the seldom rains the air turns
From the color of browned butter
Into a window through which I may see
All the way from here to my boyhood.
I am able to make out the landmarks
Of all my childish adventures:
The funny mound in the middle of the landscape
From where the Indians use to send signals;
The islands, all named for saints, and tiny
Figures arrayed by a semi-arid
Desert next to the sea—
Gulls wheeling over prickly pear cactus—
Hills made green by artifice and imported water.

My vantage point is a cat-bird seat
Up in the western entrance to a broken bowl of hills,
Which were once a long weekend ride
From the city where I grew up.

(O, Indiana by the sea!)

Driving for hours through heady perfume,
Orange groves sprinkled with little towns now sewn
Together into a neon quilt sprawling all the way

From La Ciudad de la Reina de Los Angeles, God help us,
All the way to this place, where I live, which the city fathers
Have decided to call
The New Mayberry.

This is my sixty third lap around the sun, aboard a ball
Inside a bowl, within a basin. I realize now
The eye-burning murk which is the trademark of the place
Preceded the Indians, the Spaniards, the Indianians,
It just *was* even in the time of the happy aboriginals, who called
This "The valley of smokes"
The sea is a constant, too, one wet
Coup de torchon, whereon I may scribble my script—
Past, present, even
My possible future.

Camera Lucida

We followed the front, east-north-east,
Against the caveat of the Boss, who said
Traffic would be terrible. Wrong. Four hours
From here to lawlessness, also known as Nevada.
After a night of sleep and cheap eats at Whiskey Pete's
We wend our way across that nondescript landscape
Into one of the states that Crazy Dave says ought to be
Quarantined—Utah—the other being, by the way,
Colorado.

The red flow of the Virgin
River, and the beautifully tortured
Geology of the river's gorge
Become for me the real entrance
To our trip.

Consider this overture:
The eerily beautiful shapes of Zion at twilight;
The fantasy landscape of Bryce in sunlight, after snow;
The monolithic quality of Capitol Reef, in latelight.
Our campsite on the way to Gemini Bridges, with the moon,

The La Sals, and Canyonlands next to us:
Islands in the Sky.

Consider this theme:
Do we stay here in the "Valley of Smokes"
Or move to the old French trapper town
To make a new life.

Consider this denouement:
Passing through to the coast
And all those breathtaking vistas
I think about a poem I want to call
Big Sur, The Oranges of Hieronymus Bosch, and Thou.

These are the gifs, jpegs, and bitmaps of our trip.
Photography will always fail us, for cameras
Can't see the same thing our eyes do; our eyes
Can't see the same thing our minds do, and our minds
Cannot see.

airplane poem

like tin pushers sitting in darkened rooms—
the better to see the green spokes circling
the screens, the better to wrangle
the calculus of transponders in motion—
watching, hushed, while
little alphanumeric scribbles
representing unbelievable amounts
of metal and flesh flying at high altitude
and speed, tick their incremental way
across a video game version of flight.

a hundred years from kittyhawk
to here, darling, where we live
beneath these aerial pathways.

remember in the barrio, how the roar
of inbound to LAX bothered us less
than the loud late-night mariachi wafting
on the weed-scented breeze,
or the occasional drive-by bullets?
while three blocks away
behind the invisible barriers of their
manicured lawns, the well to do worried
more about plummeting property values
than airplanes falling from the sky.

how oddly fitting that our address
and fortunes have changed—
yet our circumstance remains similar.

now the roar of inbound to john wayne airport
is the whitenoise we've grown accustomed to
up here on our hill, above the taquerias,
the carnecerias, the noise and graffiti
of all those sweet brown people
who pray god into their cinder block and wrought
iron walled yards full of cars
to protect them
from falling airplanes and from
the whites who live above them
like tin pushers sitting in darkened rooms.

The Workmen

for Alan Michael Parker

Just before the workmen, worthy of their hire,
come into view, they are announced by strange melody
and syncopation—the rising and percussive songs
of nails, like questions; the descending arias
of saws, like answers. The rat-a-tat of nail guns
in a rhythm section repetition:
shave and a hair cut, shave and a hair cut—
the very music of Vishnu and Shiva,
personified in hardware.

A woman, sunbathing naked on the roof, gazes out
into the sky's thin sea, watching clouds scud by
like schooners. A woman who, between the din and drum
becomes a tuned fork, tines humming to the whine of saws,
thrumming to the drums of hammers.
And the workmen, worthy of their hire, become aroused
at the sight of skin, that world, that sea of skin, into the which
they each and all wish now to be drowned.
And gravity fails, in a localized manner.
And the naked woman rises, in a profane annunciation.
And the workmen, worthy of their hire,
stare into the future and begin to speak in tongues.

Seven Metamorphoses from Syrup to Strange Flight

1.

Last year, when you were in the kitchen,
mostly naked,
studying to become a tree,
I was in the yard,
pencil tip to tongue,
awaiting lightning.
Now you are, cum laude,
aspen, quaking, warm dewdrops of summer
morning draping all your slender limbs.
(Soft flesh, not wood you are, I wrote)
and I am still this
love-struck scribbler.

2.

When you ceased to be a banker
I renounced my life of crime,
but not until I held you up.
I had to take you hostage
in order to make
a clean getaway.

3.

When I am a painter,
you are all the cool colors

of my palette:
malachite, lapis, cerulean, green,
swirling burgundy down
into your favorite—
royal purple.

4.

If you were the painter
I would be all the warm:
sienna, umber, ochre, blood,
alazarin and autumn gold.

5.

We are complementary,
chromatically and temperamentally.

6.

If if is is,
maybe becomes be.
Tenuous turns tensile,
almost morphs to most,
and all these ifs of you,
and all those whens of me,
burn to ash, and from that pyre comes this weird phoenix:

7.

We.

Letter to the Doctor, or, the Lycanthropes Lament

Rumor has it you're resorting
to your pipes and syringes again, your world
contracted from planet sized
where your friends are all at large,
into a fist-sized ball of opish. Little brown orb
where it is always summer, under an albino sun;
where there is no place for regret,
and all the pretty girls and boys
       are required by custom to go naked,
            so that the wearing of clothes is shameful.

Symptomatology, mine which only occurs
when the moon is full, and the dew upon the grass,
monthly, like some weird repeating menarche
involving other's blood.

Yours, catalyzed by almost anything, a word, a star, a photograph,
happens at random times and places. The outcome is the same—
both of us oblivious to morals, mores, conventions—

both of us loping through the streets, unclad,

laughing.

I am no longer safe even in sunlight. Nor are those around me.
Those nearest me.
You have never been safe. Nor have those who've loved you.

I write, I suppose, to let you know your diagnosis was correct.
To ask you for a word, some hope, perhaps a silver bullet,
if you ever come back from the haze.

Keep in touch, I must go now, I can hear the moon.

Poem under the influence
for Matthew Rohrer

The candlestick beneath the stairs
plugged its ears and sang a tune to cover
the sound of the chandelier gagging.

Inter-racial affairs went on among the mismatched
dining room chairs.

A white pine Scandinavian modern
shamelessly pressed its leg against
a cherry wine skinned Windsor.

The old blender, canvassing for the upcoming election,
had pissed itself. Mr. Coffee
and the toaster, tittered, down at the end
of the counter—figures, a *Republican*.

Upstairs, all the books in the library
sighed.

The radio alarm clock
declared a wildcat strike,
causing the hapless homeowners
to be late for work.

Later,
over dinner,
they thought it odd
that both of them had dreamt
the sky rained
men in overcoats and bowler hats.

Jade Blue

Solar flares
and proton storms,
noctilucent breakers, the happy resolution
of recurring dreams, and a chance meeting—all share
the hue of Buddha's Seventh Stone,
blue-green.

Once, on a midnight walk in Arizona,
he witnessed the once-in-a-century
appearance at that latitude
of the Aurora Borealis. At first
he thought the mountains were on fire,
until he saw that curtain in the sky
turn slowly to

the perfect color
of the first time he saw surf light up at night,
on Venice Beach, at five a.m., in 1962.
Searching for the Holy Barbarians, who'd already
made their exit to San Francisco. He
stumbled across the sand, to find
that all the waves were luminous,
glowing with

the perfect color
of the final installment

of his recurring childhood dream.
Swept overboard in a storm,
he would always startle awake; *that* time
he found to his delight that he could breathe
underwater. He swam as graceful as a fish,
while the storm raged on above him.
Untouched by trouble. At peace.
In a warm and welcoming sea

the perfect color
of her eyes, that day
when she first said
she loved him.

Venus & Mars

She comes like mist
caressing coastal hills
to kiss the sea.

He wants to bump
and grind together like
tectonic plates.

Her soundtrack swells
with violins, French horns, and
tinkling bells.

He is cranking up a
bottom heavy groove—
the neighbors are complaining.

Her eyes are the color
of the sky above
a non-existent country.

His are brown.

She would like to go
for a slow Sunday drive.

He wants to skip the break-in

period, take the inline six
out for a test drive
in her hills.

She is
Botticelli's Venus.

He is
Dogs Playing Cards.

She is a mystery
basket of contradictions.

He—a walking volume
of explanations.

She wants dinner at sunset,
candlelight
and wine.

He is happiest
scarfing potato chips
in the blue light of the TV
with a beer.

She is so in touch
with her feelings.

His are radioed in

from his home planet,
with an eighteen hour delay.

She is Vogue.

He is Guns and Ammo.

He sometimes says
he wants her
to have his children.

She often wonders
how
the species manages to survive.

Cowboys & Indians

Just here, where grid gives way
to igneous rock, and manicured lawns
surrender to bunch grass and cattle tracks,
we live in a pueblo built to code.

This is what's left of the old west:

The tree where the posse hung Juan Flores
and his outlaw band, stands near a man-made lake
stocked with trout and over run with hobby fishermen.
Weekend outlaws roar past on $50,000.00 Harleys
frightening the fish.

To our north, there is a traffic signal
with a mounted sign which reads: Horse Xing.
A button fastened high on the pole
so affluent cowgirls needn't dismount to press it.

To the west, where the Indians live,
demarking their reservation with runic symbols
written in spray-paint on every cinder block wall,
day workers cluster in the drug store parking lot.

(Is it better to assimilate and serve than to die?)

To the south is an airport
with a 12 foot statue in the terminal—
John Wayne, frozen mid-stride in that cattywampus
walk of his, overseeing arrivals and departures.

To the east where a big ranch sits—
last vestige of the old days and the old ways,
the last round-up was done to make way
for subdivisions.

I am a cowboy without a horse, and my gun
is tucked away somewhere in a sock drawer.

Childhood Aspirations

When I was a boy
I was a bird interpreter,
translating every dialect
of chirp and twitter.

When I was a little older
I never really wanted to be
a doctor,
lawyer,
butcher,
baker,
big deal maker. Instead, a
paleontologist, digging up dinosaurs,
exposing evolutionary newspapers
in splintered patterns
of bone.

When I was a boy
I was polymathically perverse.
I wished to be an astronomer,
charting the constellations
of freckles
between girls' breasts.

I never really wanted
To be a policeman, or a fireman, instead
      I wanted to fly
      I wanted to be naked
      I wanted to see women in disarray
      I wanted to be pathological liar
      I wanted the moon to be my lover
      I wanted to be copper-
      skinned and cool,
      I wanted to play
the trumpet.

When I was a boy
I was a bird interpreter. Even though I knew

there would *never* be any money in it.

House Sitting (a "B" movie)
for Amélie Frank

1.

The Monahans are in Europe,
leaving les objets du papier,
two ancient dogs and two
patrician cats in your care—

it's late, the sylph
is sleeping, and we

(employing laughter)

have achieved the specific gravity
of children—two human balloons
with our backs and feet
against the cottage cheese ceiling.

We bump and nuzzle,
compare notes on the feng shui
of the room and fly into fits
at the cat's astonished stares.

Here:

hours minutes and boundaries

have become meaningless.

Here:

everything is waveform and wingbeat;
we speak the Shibboleth;
we know the semiotic semaphore.

Here:

2.

Yours, Sister-Friend,
is the peculiar grace and tenderness
of freight trains—

the sheer tonnage of sorrow

in your tow is so stupendous—
your grasp of night-song
so nonpareil.

I commend myself
for uncoupling you from these
however temporarily. And as for me
these visits

to a childhood neither of us had
leave me breathless

as the boy I never was and wanting

more.

3.

We put each other on (and off)
like costumes.
We visit empty envelopes,

or burn them and scatter the ashes.

We laugh,

until the isness of everything
sideswipes us again;
things take weight
and we fall to the floor—

cinematically.

Ars Poetica

There are lemon slices and lily pads in the waters of the pond. Rocks peek out of cracks in the boxes, and bees are busy in the weeds. At the park on the Street of Clocks men are reading the spaces *between* the words of their books, and chess masters at the benches play backwards. Tie-dyed shamans divine our future, and study our past. Our term for far, far away (in the lingua franca) is: "there, where a child cries mother, mother!" Our word for here is: "here." Eternity exists in a heartbeat; the multiverse within your pretty sister. There is a bordello in the basement of our church, frogs and crawdads in our aqueducts, and fire hydrants have taken to pissing on the dogs. There is mariachi music, and the cordite cologne of live ammo, on the yesca scented breeze. Hep cats sit in the windowsills, sniffing. Small brown men walk around whistling. Mormons ring the doorbells two by two. In the morning, songbirds sing so loudly the pictures on the walls go off kilter. Nightly, we are serenaded by sirens. Everywhere, all around us, there is breathtaking beauty—which seems to be the reason the newest fad is suicide. Our mathematicians do the Macarena; our theologians do the Antler Dance. Our philosophers are all hollering: "Ollie, Ollie Otsin, free, free, free!" By day we work the mines. At night we sleep in the whorls of our lovers fingerprints.

Highway 39 Revisited

There was a big commotion down at the Bistro,
over some dame, a broad, this chick, who
in the Sex & Love Addicts Anonymous literature
would be someone to whom
magical powers were attributed.

She was fussing over an old-fashioned
beatnik, new-fangled upstart, post-
post-post-modern
dialectical immaterialist, who wore
on his sleeve, his heart, which resembled
nothing,
so much as a magnesium fire.

He had the look of a 3 time loser,
gazing upon liberty for the last time
while they threw the book at him
for spitting on the sidewalk.

She seemed like the last chance for gasoline
before 40 years in the wilderness.

Carried herself like royalty, with a cigarette in her mouth
and a scotch, neat, in her hand.

Together, they behaved like
George and Marion Kirby, after the car crash; like
Julius and Ethel Rosenberg, before the breaker was thrown; like
John Cusack's marionette versions of Abelarde and Eloise.

They were so beautiful, in a violent kind of way.

Around them people wailed
and rent their garments, scattered ashes
upon each other's heads, sang threnodies. Outside
an armed robbery took place in plain sight. And somewhere
poems yawned and rubbed the sleep out of their eyes.

What's in a name?

Hana Lena Luakalimahina Audreyana Ackerman Schwartz-Ismail
doesn't
want to know the secret name
God has written upon a white stone
and saves for her in heaven. She has plenty of trouble
handling the handle she already has.

A one woman multi-culture, Miss Lu (as she is known
for short) loves the feel and shape of words—
their bodily pleasure—the very sound of *language*,
the word for words, is itself so sensuous to her
she warms slightly when it rolls across her
palette, lips, teeth and tongue.

But personal names, please God, and thank you,
no more personal names. Unless it might be one which is
a synthesis of signifier and signified,
a spatial and conceptual sfumato,
a semiotic necessity, if you will.

Hana Lena is part Crow. She sits
cornerwise across the table from
a South Eastern Cherokee,

a reluctant Deutschlander, and
a watered down Scot. All of whom
occupy the same body.

With a offhand élan, she gives this man
a pair of eyes with which to see
himself. He returns the favor. In the process,
in the Native American way, they have exchanged
secret names,

each one two pages long, single spaced, and dense
with mirrors—meaning—melody.
Revealing these names in their entirety
to the world at large would kill their powers.

To conceal them completely would leave us without and ending. So here:

part of hers for him meant: elven;
part of his for her meant: sister.

Suicide Pantoum

All memories are made of tears.
*—from the film **2046***

Like Van Gogh scratching at the lobe of a phantom ear,
our tongues worry the gristle of memory in the mind's teeth—
the shrapnel in our hearts—the knowledge that our days are numbered.
We prospect for some passable facsimile of summer.

Our tongues worry the gristle of memory in the mind's teeth:
images of women in dishabille, presenting like mares in heat.
We prospect for some passable facsimile of summer—
glycerin and liquid crystal displays—in lieu of Sugar Plum Faeries.

Images of women in dishabille presenting like mares in heat—
time's thieves, iron pyrite, fool's cure for the common burden. All these
glycerin and liquid crystal displays—in lieu of Sugar Plum Faeries.
Ah, Judas is in all of us, selling off Emmanuel for trinkets.

Time's thieves, iron pyrite, fool's cure for the common burden, all these
winter days wasted in the service of the sarx, the weight.
Ah, Judas is in all of us, selling off Emmanuel for trinkets,
seeking remedies for rancor, anodynes for ennui, magic bullets.

Winter days wasted in the service of the sarx. The weight,
the shrapnel in our hearts, the knowledge that our days are numbered,
seeking remedies for rancor, anodynes for ennui, magic bullets—
like Van Gogh scratching at the lobe of a phantom ear.

Santiago Canyon

for Jamie O'Halloran

Crossing Horsethief Wash, riding home
into the westering sun, the last blades of light
show the hills flayed open to make roads.
Beneath their skins of buckwheat,
black sage and prickly pear, the muscle
is the color of cooked salmon.

We live near the bottom
of a bowl of hills.

Our lives are fragile scripts
written upon cosmic dust
and dead skin.

Ghosts are lumbering through our dreams.

~~

Katalpa, former dwelling place of Chiningchinish,
is now a forest of microwave towers.
The displaced god now wanders the lowlands—
frightening white men.

We are like the immigrant trees,
all leaning the direction
of the prevailing wind.

Small brown men walk upright amongst us,
whistling.

Weights & Measures

I wax astrologic, crustacean, at the mercy of tides.
You wane practical, a voice emanating from a pair of scales.
"Come out. When will you come out of your shell?"
you ask. Whenever you stop your infernal weighing.
I am a fun-house hall of mirrors. You are a vernier, a compass, an abacus.
Perhaps a paradigm shift would help us find harmony. The Chinese

Zodiac says Sheep and Boar are a favorable pairing. In Chinese
Astrology a Boar would never answer to the lunar pull of tides;
a Sheep would have no use for plumb-bobs, or abaci,
theodolites, calipers, micrometers, much less a pair of scales.
Glad the Boar in a world with no measures, no weighing.
Happy the Sheep whose mate wears no shell.

Year of the Sheep. Year of the Boar. Myself *sans* shell,
forfeiting my wonderful exoskeleton to morph into a Chinese
Pig? Easier to see you as ewe. Though now I am weighing—
that very Libran thing which turned the tides
eastward in the first place—in hopes of ditching scales,
rods, rulers, sextants, levels, loglines, the nonius, the abacus,

et alia. Go north! Where our fingers and toes become abaci
of flesh, counting order out of chaos; where this shell
of mine is not mandated by stars. Then we'd see, the scales
falling from our eyes, the Alder and the Chinese
tree outside our window, dancing in the thin tide

of atmosphere are key. Let us cease weighing

the formula of froth to check compatibility. Begin instead weighing
our respective places in the Green Way. Scrap your abacus
and take our measure by these trees swaying in air's tides.
To be patient as an Alder, I'd give up my shell.
To grow strong and slow alongside a slender Chinese
Elm, symmetrical as scales

which measure only atmosphere, I could grow bark, like scales,
in place of my crust. If you could see your way in
to keep the sun, but not it's signs, we would eschew Chinese
Astrology too, in favor of this old druidic way. Abacus
be damned. "When will you ever come out of your shell?"
you ask. When the tides

have turned forever against all measuring. When the tides
oppose all weighing—I will emerge from my shell,
not crab, pig, tree—but man, when you become my woman,
instead of a goddamn scale.

Mexican Holiday

1. The Big Kahuna

Something rode his heart so hard
parts of his skin turned
adamantine, then cracked
open like dry riverbed,
deep into the living meat.

That pain was the price he paid
to find a perfect curl
down at the bottom of the bluff,
in a limpid arc of green
where he could lose himself
to become beauty.

2. Scarecrow Crazy Jeff

Jeffrey's cheeks are the most intricate atlas
of roads to nowhere; the geography changes
when he smiles.

When unseen, we presumed him to be
in the company of the people
he'd picked up at sea,
Dorsey, Dorsala, Orcetta,
poltergeists with a penchant
for destroying household appliances.

We last saw him outside, dancing in the sand,
Margarita raised to the sun.
He used to be a cloud, but tendered resignation
when he was demoted
from a downpour to a drizzle.

He was contemplating a career move,
thinking of becoming a wave.

3. *The Poet*

Foolish boy thought he had all his demons at bay,
failing to notice the expiration date
on his protective amulet had already passed.
Sauntered over the border, straight into a fracas
with the Philistines.

At the posh resort
all the waiters were pistoleros. Our boy was armed
only with his poetry. The pen
may be mightier than the sword,
but it's no match for a .357

"If it wasn't for this freaking haircut" he muttered,
doing a frantic boxstep
in methamphetamine time, while bullets
whined around him like bees.

The money launderers had a good laugh
at the last line of his book.

unpunctuated tercets
ending with haiku

at a loping gait we catch up
with the subject of this sentence
the third millennium

a tertiary parenthesis
playing bumpercars
with its brothers or possibly

the third of those monkey statues or then again it could be
the smokebound eastern seaboard
of a triptych by Hieronymus Bosch

you may notice our voices echoing
when we speak inside the hill
blown up to build this place

this peaceful feeling
is the kirlian residue
of that thirty million year old stone

(breath)

we are divining our future
in the vermicular calligraphy of the sun
dried night crawlers on the sidewalk

studying our past
in the mating patterns of raptors and the mourning

doves nesting outside our window

wishing we were hollow
boned and alate   fertile as these smug
birds returning in an unseasonable spring

(exhalation)

according to prevailing theory
the planet is a pirate ship
manned by chaos finest contraptions

a loose knit crew
flaunting the second law of thermodynamics
exchanging high fives and piña coladas

while they commit mass suicide as art
poke holes in the ionosphere
make swiss cheese of the protective force field above them

while they raze the trees
that breath the gas that blows the bellows
which fires the coals

of life on a ball that chance built
or again this could be
all by design   like

smooth rivers washing
all of our sorrows down to
oceans made of tears

The Gold Rush of 1949

A hollow cane full of candy,
the fall down the stairs. Uncle Harry
and the airplanes with collapsible wings.
The snowdrifts outside, and a television
as huge as post-war prosperity, with a saucer
sized screen, delivering Froggy—
plunking his magic twanger, and fucking
with Andy Devine.

This was in the East.

The DeSoto, they told me, was named
"The Green Hornet."
American looked like the backside of a front
seat, the inside
of a sick bag. There was a killer
on the road. A dark refrain
woven into a sparkling chorus.

This was our opus.

The Bisbee rancher only paid
minimum wage, so it was on to California,
where a magazine salesman
married an Indian woman,
after discovering gold. Men still wore sidearms
out in the open, 100 years after the goldrush.

This was in the West.

Out there, there were bats
in the attic, deer on the lawn, the smell of dynamite
at the adit. Out there, there were mornings
which called for some sort of ship
to navigate the cotton ball sea
of clouds between the island mountains.

Out in the shining West.

Father was on the green chain, days;
evenings and weekends he was sinking
a drift into a promising quartz sprinkled
outcrop of rock. Mother wore blasting caps
in her gloves fingertips (once!). And she was
beautiful.

This is the Truth.

After Old Man Kelly's fighting cock
tried to peck a hole into my head
I understood all the languages
of birds and animals;
which I have since forgotten.

After Old Man Kelly tried to put
his withered cock into my sister,
she understood all the lunacy
of men and nations;
which she has since remembered.

These are our Sorrows.

So how shall we end this poem?
Shall I tell you
how a man gives up
his dreams of fortune
to save his little family?

Pas de Deux

Mother was an artist's model, once.
Father worked his life in steel.

My dad could chin himself
two-fingered, on the doorframe
(and *did*, when he was drunk).

My mom could make plants sprout and grow
from sprigs she collected
on afternoon walks.
Father could draw a perfect likeness,
but had no truck with the artist's life.

Mother shed her clothes,
posing nude for a bronze statue
which stands somewhere
in Pennsylvania
at the edge of a reflecting pool.

My father was not the sculptor.
(*Walking on the beach in Mexico,*

with a bad case of the blues,
I saw the shells of mollusks
so beautiful they looked like jewelry)

Mother was an artist's model, once.

My father's ships still ply the sea.
My mother's statue stands by a pool,

arms raised, as if waiting
for the sky to send a cleansing rain.

Sans Envoi

Poor mother's heart
would hit a wind shear, each time another
red flannel shirt wore a new man
into the room. Spiral into a dream
where she had seen that shirt
on a stranger. Never

seeing his face, never
so much as exchanging a word, her heart
had become a sextant, the red shirted
man her lodestar. Another man
(our father) owned her day, her dream
belonged to this ephemeral man

who loved her more purely than any man
in all her waking life. She never
revisited that dream.
Its weight upon her heart
the only evidence of another
kind of love. The common cloth of that shirt,

simple workingman's shirt,
was her only clue to the man.
So, each time she saw it on another

(it was never him
only his insignia) her heart
would spin into a daydream

of love. Her face, in this dream,
would rest upon the front of his shirt,
and she could feel the beating of his heart,
this man
whom she had never
seen. But it was always just another

man, ordinary and real. Another
flawed human, drawn by the cloth of his own dream.
Poor mother was never
allowed to rest her head upon that shirt.
Never, in this lifetime, actually saw the man
who truly owned her heart.

El Dia de los Muertos

The day latinos remember their dead,
luminarias everywhere, skeletons
dancing in the street, and the dead
smoking cigarettes and smiling.

Asian homes are densely packed
with ancestors, ghosts shoulder to shoulder
so thick, six or seven generations
are passed through when the living
walk from one room to another.

Samhain is the root of Halloween, the nearest
thing we white folks have to venerating
the departed, gone, all but forgotten. Doorbells
ring, little goblins deliver smudged telegrams
from the other side.

What of me and mine, rootless, who can barely
recall the names of those who came before, let alone
celebrate them? If only we had more memories,
recipes, photographs. Some artifacts to anchor
us to *now*, to inform us of where we are from,
who we are.

Now each of the miles which separate me
from my grandchildren is a sorrow to their
mother's hearts, my daughters, who never knew
their grandparents, who don't know
their family tree.

But the departed are nearer than breath, according
to those other cultures, so possibly, on some windless
days
my grandchildren's hair get mussed
by their great
great
grandparent's hands.

Inquiry to Hoopy
for Matthew R. and Jeff C.

Who could say whether or not you trifled with God's
affections when you left for the frontier. We were
appalled at the lack of fanfare for your departure. These
bumpkins must know that few receive the opportunity,
the requisite equipment, much less the funding, to
monitor the heartbeat of a star.

What is the atmosphere like there? Where we are
stationed it has the color and consistency of browned
butter.

When is your re-entry scheduled? We need your ETA
so we may know when to get tickets for the traveling
Brueghel exhibit. The countess says peasant dances
always remind her of you.

Where will you bivouac? With Mr. Rohrer? Mr. Clark?
How shall we know where to send this bloody steamer
truck of yours, which reeks of opium and glowing coals?

Why do we write? Dearest Hoopster, forgive us for
opening an old wound, but you never seemed quite
the same after the little door slid back and the Padre
gave you such short shrift, and this on the eve of your
departure!

How could we have known he was one of those tipsy
Benedictines? Hoopy, the question on everyone's lips is:
have you found absolution yet?

SOME THOUGHTS ABOUT 56 YEARS OF EXISTENCE

after Jeff Clark
after Henri Michaux

As for man, his days are like grass;
as a flower of the field, so he flourishes,
when the wind has passed over it, it is no more;
and its place acknowledges it no longer.
Psalm 103:15,16

1947

Is a wonderful year for Cadillacs.
J'arrive, sans culotte! Tiny feckless galoot, disappointment
at the outset (they wanted a girl); destined, nevertheless, to be
as wonderful and vulgar as America.
Born at the confluence of waters: Allegheny, Ohio,
and Monongahela. Son of redbloods—strophe:
Mom was Rosie the Riveter; Father was G.I.Joe—antistrophe:

We were a molly-coddle, all the same.

1948

We learned the narrow escape, the plea bargain;
unlearned the dim remnants and vestiges of other dimensions. Ours
was the particular sadness of the involuntarily disenfranchised.

1949

Q: Ou sont les neiges d'antan? A: Piled outside the front door,
thank you.
Uncle Harry lived up in the attic, building airplanes.
The Gold Bug bit Dad. Badly. All we can remember
is cathode rays and spilled candy.

1950

Shoe-horned into a green DeSoto, and schlepped, willy-nilly,
across the continent.

1951

Miss Salquist became the Queen of All Sorrows.
We discovered our penis.
Satan lived in a duplex on the corner, looking
remarkably like a black cocker-spaniel.
There was a witch (or so we thought) two doors down,
who gave out cups of lucky pennies on Halloween.
The ground cracked open one morning and
Mother drank iodine. After her stomach was pumped,
she gave her heart to Christ.

1952

O, Iowa by the sea!

1953

In the schoolyard, staring rapt at Miss Allen's hips,
and the soft contrapuntal metronome of her ponytail,
precocious boy begins to dream of rendezvous
in water towers—frightening revelations
in underground mazes.

1954

The gap-toothed knuckle-buster (who was once a dashing boy)
fashioned his arms into a drydock, suspending us over the ocean.
We learned fear and wonder, in three feet of water.

1955

St. Donna of the dimples, of the blue, blue eyes
had us arrested and detained for kissing her without permit.
We rediscovered our penis, invented the transmogrifier, began composing
poems which would not be committed to paper until 40 years later.

1956—1959

Our sister eloped with a fisherman. Our best friend moved away—
no forwarding address. Mother had signs of schizophrenia with
delusions of persecution. Loss,
loss, confusion; these became the recurring pattern.

1960

Lust arrived like virulence on a cellular level.
Love was like a sky lousy with clouds.

1961

Nadya Keenoy's legs.

1962

Evil companions arrived like welcome reinforcements. It felt
good to be bad.

1963

Ionesco al fresco. We mecca to the spot where the hipsters lived.
3:00 a.m. Ocean shoulders loom moonless, lit from within.
And all the beats are gone man, real gone...

1964

Is the edge of a precipice over which we stare nervously.

1965

Strange rays emanate from the little white clapboard
house across the street. Mother is given *vision* and sees
the sinister beams wash over the heads of her loved ones
as they sit in the kitchen telling ghost stories over coffee.
Her boy falls in love with the moon. Father goes along
as though nothing has happened

1966

We hitch-hiked across the surface of the sun.

1967

When that gangster (wannabe) from Boston stood over
us, holding a book from the nightstand, he turned
to the surfer (Director of the United Federation of

Nightcrawling Amphibians) and pronounced us the founding citizen of our own fantasy world.

1968

First thoughts of suicide.

1969

First suicide. (Failed).

1970

The study of comparative religion was undertaken. This began with the purchase of platform shoes and bell-bottom pants. Transcendental Meditation was a bust. After paying fruit, flowers, and a week's pay for a syllable, it was revealed that ours, our ex-room mates, and Kurt Vonnegut's mantra were all the same. It was:

....

....

....

1971

A small hand opened a door.

1972

The God of Abraham, Isaac, and Jacob
dropped in at a potluck dinner in Costa Mesa,
saran wrap over a bowl of manna.

1973

Strutting and preening like some clown Quixote, that
addiction to "The Softness" begins.

1974

A compact package arrives: incubated, intubated,
bathed in strange light. One lung collapsed, blood
volume low; one tiny foot in this world—the other in
that other realm where our twin sisters, stillborn, went.

1975

1976

1977

Another package arrives, so well-formed, while divorce rears its ugly head.

1978

1979

She who was once the shipwright's beautiful wife was coated in gold salts, taken by cancer. After heroic measures failed, we were summoned. The last sight of Mother was with wig and dentures removed, a toothless, shriveled figure, mouth open in a silent scream.

1980

1981

1982

1983

1984

Orwell's prediction failed to materialize, so we
purchased a sports car.

1985

1986

1987

1989—1991

Three years to holy to profane on the page.

1992

After seven years in the doldrums, any wind is welcome,
even widdershins.

1993

Dr. Grip, the Pilot, informs the passengers
that the voyage will resume, as soon
as the composition of the hull can be determined:
    fiberglass,
    ferro-cement,
    fine wood,
    or gold…

1994

Thanks be to that Merrimac woman, whose love wounds
are like road flares, pointing not away, but toward
the crash.

1995

An old man looks up,
across the face of the moon
translucent clouds move.

1996

That last stanza was a haiku.

1997

A dark blue low flying UFO is sighted
sweeping around the curve of the Sadao S. Munimori
memorial interchange.

1998

Is the face of the precipice we make our new home on.

1999

The women carry my sins, like sacks full of rocks
between their breasts. My slow death, come time for the stoning,
is to watch them fling these at each other, until they bleed.

2000

Prozac becomes *the* fin du siecle panacea.

2001

They fail to find that monolith on the moon.

2002

The composition of the hull is finally determined. The
radio-woman, Sparks, declares
the ship "differently commanded." Dr. Grip, the Pilot,
instructs the engine room:
all ahead full.

2003

Nous arrivons, maintenant avec culotte, et maintenant
avec cette pensée irrécusable:
all that we truly possess
is this moment.

Brief Encounters

Bump against these home-spun
holy men, hard-wired to run contrary,
and most seem as though something
has brought every nerve
screaming to the surface of their skin
like drowning swimmers.

The authorities usually want to institutionalize them.
Their families usually think it necessary too.
God's mom, if you recall, wanted to have *him*
under 72 hours of observation. So it shouldn't
surprise deity in the least when his chosen
behave like time lapse films
running backwards, speaking
in the tongues of men and angels, seeing
reality peel away like veneers.

Observe these paragons of plaster,
the heroes of the faith:
adulterers, drunks, murderers, liars, connivers,
polygamists, practitioners of incest, schemers,
madmen, the whole gamut from
manic-depressives to OCDs—all prey
to the full spectrum of waverings and doubts,
And take hope—
for when the catalog of sins
is shouted from the rooftops
and the fuel of hell is revealed to be
an infinite supply of little pellets
made of shame, take heart, take heart
O ye of little faith, and less rectitude—
you have been chosen.

My Guidebook to Beatdom

was a paperback book of cartoons
       as was
that unread copy of The Holy Barbarians
       as was
my dog-eared copy of The Subterraneans.
              My map to the land of hip was
a poster in a shop that was never open
       as was
that cornball poem in The Village Voice—
       (Beat be ben zootism
            Kerouac ben zooter
               Take off your clothes
                  Climb on your scooter)
       as was
that lexicon of slang terms from
         77 Sunset Strip, finger snap, finger snap.
        As was
the black and white picture of a hipster in blue jeans
       and huaraches, a beat fashion statement, as
were the black stockings Anet Welsh wore
       as was
the corduroy coat I used to wear
       as was
all the Red Mountain wine we drank,
       as were
all those brain cells which died from all the Red
         Mountain wine we drank.
My baedeker to beatdom
       was you.

Sargasso

I was asked to write a treatise on horizons.

Call this research:
watching Lost Horizon,
listening to Vertical Horizon.
reading Split Horizon,
and spending time in the doldrums.

Sufficient time for *all* the cells in my body to renew.

I was asked by a person in my own employ,
whose job was to torture me, to submit
a baedeker to the meetings
of ocean and sky.

When I could no longer hold water, and my thoughts
had become thin as clouds, this attempt:

For seven years the vessel barely rocked.
No problem with the engine,
she was simply under the direction of a captain
with no sense of direction. Small comfort
for the passengers, who kept looking at their watches.

There were births, marriages, funerals; generations

coming in and passing away. Isolated in the slow rhythm
of the sun describing arcs
above a concrete sea.

Truth be told—there was no voyage.
Truth be told—there was no vessel.
Only a land-locked trope. Truth:
I was both the ship and the clueless captain.
But the person paid to torture me was very real.

My report:

Horizons are illusory.
The meeting of the oceans and the skies
only occurs during rain, drops falling
like letters on a page.

Call me captain. Come aboard.

Clothespin angel smiling

sleepy eyed after loving
lips parted
as sumptuously
as a Gustav Klimt kiss
she
reluctantly
barebacks into the day
later
in the park
she's dancing
under a jackaranda
small lavender colored
parachutes
spiraling down
into her hands
we walk
along the shore of the lake
the back of her hand
brushes reeds
my shaking thighs
iridescent dragonflies

like jeweled engines
mate mid-flight
over white and gold explosions
water lilies
there is a little girl
upon the pier
her brothers cast lines
while she casts
her bread upon the water
and everything
speaks
in the mystery
language
of our loins

Paper Boat

From bow
to stern the beams
and strakes
were ripped by rocks
and licked by sea tongues,

that sweet wood now imbued
with salty tang.

The captain sprawled
ragdollwise
on the fever dream
of a shore
uncharted;

scattered with pale
shattered logs,
the sun
bleached bones
of other ships.

A cluster of natives,
naked ministering angels,
made sails
of their skin, ropes
of their hair, and with
spit, blood, and sweat
they rebuilt his boat

and he, better than before.

Then bid him go,
you are home now,

stay.

Post Mortem

When love dies,
whether from foul play, natural causes,
disuse, or simple neglect
the authorities come in.

There is always an evidentiary outline,
but no crime
scene tape to keep the curious
from trampling over the clues.

Everyone becomes an amateur
coroner-for-a-day.
If this, if that. Too bad. Tsk tsk.
Speculations hopping around like carrion crows.

When love dies, the real
authorities are never called
in for crimes of the heart occur
outside of jurisprudence.

There is always an outline,
but no body to be seen,
though they exist—
these *corpora delecti*—

as any former lover will attest.
In fact we drag them around with us,
their weight slowing us down, and hurting
like the phantom limbs of amputees.

Project for Nightgaunt

I came across a moss colored cocktail
made of homesickness and dread
at Bela Lugosi's last known address—
there to feed the cats of a friend.

The longest trip I ever took
was from a television to a strange bed,
my first night away from home,
after watching Dracula implode
when a stake was driven through his heart.

The willing suspension of disbelief is easy when you are ten years old.

Now I find the collective unconscious flickers
like early cinema, goofing on the
Transylvanian patois, and the penetrating gaze
Bela traded to become a monster, his meme
writ large on every white screen.

Now I shiver, imagining a figure
staring up at the window from the street below—
darkness blooming from his shoulders
and spreading like a cape—bat shaped
and as big as the Hollywood night.

11:11

Do we compose poems?
Or do the poems, themselves possessing mind, write us?
No place for cognoscenti this—
everything but sawdust on the floor—
this is the old-time religion.

Which of your sons, if he asked of his father
a drink of water, would receive a baseball cap?
Or for an appliance, would receive instead
an explanation of the significance of flowers
in still life painting?

Here at the church of the living word
we conduct the exegesis of the ineffable
from the license plates of automobiles. We make
uplifting homilies from empty jars, and parse
the syntax of sunlight.

Can I get an amen?

Before today's sermon, my beloved, a confession:

I have sinned, brothers and sisters, repeating
bad jokes at cemeteries; dressing like
a bridesmaid for our auto-da-fés.
I have entertained impure thoughts
of the poet laureate.

What is worse, today's sermon was meant to suggest
powerfully
that Universal Love is real, and yours for the asking.
But now it has taken unto itself the ontology
of cartoons. My beloved

beware the sin the Pharisees stumbled over,

forgive me.

Dates, Feasts, Fasts, Aspects & Tide Heights

Trend forecaster and culture watcher
Faith Popcorn
says:
homeopathy
herbs, and acupuncture, and
cashing out of corporations
are in.

The Fortean Time of London reports:
incidents and sightings
of ineptitude and stupidity,
out of place animals, and falls from the sky
are up;

while genius and discovery,
crop circles and miracles,
are down.

No change in the rate of spontaneous
human combustion, or just
all around bad luck.

This just in:

a bizarre drought
of total eclipses
will soon afflict us.

About the Author

MICHAEL PAUL is the author of six chapbooks and his work has appeared in a number of literary journals including **Blue Satellite, Spillway, Pearl, Dufus** and **The Valley Contemporary Poets** anthologies. His poem *Dear Doctor* was nominated for the Pushcart Prize. He has performed at numerous venues throughout California including featured readings at both the Los Angeles and Orange County Poetry Festivals. Michael has won awards as a visual artist in several media and his paintings have been represented in fine art galleries. He currently lives in Garden Valley, California, with his wife Claudia Licht and has two daughters and four grandchildren.

ABOUT THE LUMMOX PRESS

LUMMOX Press was created in 1994 by RD Armstrong. It began as a self-publishing/DIY imprint for poetry by RD. Several chapbooks were published and in late 1995 RD began publishing the *Lummox Journal*, a monthly small/underground press lit-arts mag. Available primarily by subscription, the *LJ* continued its exploration of the "creative process" until its demise as a print mag in 2006. It was hailed as one of the best monthlies in the small press.

In 1998, Lummox began publishing the Little Red Book series, and continues to do so today. To date there are some 59 titles in the series (as of 2010) and a collection of poems from the first decade of the series has been published under the title, The Long Way Home (2009); it's a great way to explore the series.

Together with Chris Yeseta (Layout and Art Direction since 1997), RD continues to publish books that are both striking in their looks as well as their content... you'd think he was aping Black Sparrow, but he is merely trying to produce the best books he can for his clients, the poets, and their customers, you, the readers.

The following books are available directly from the Lummox Press via its website: www.lummoxpress.com or at Lummox c/o PO Box 5301, San Pedro, CA 90733. There are also E-Book (PDF) versions of most titles available. Most of these titles are available through other book sellers online, as well.

The Wren Notebook by Rick Smith (2000)

Last Call: The Legacy of Charles Bukowski
   edited by RD Armstrong (2004)

On/Off the Beaten Path by RD Armstrong (2008)

Fire and Rain—Selected Poems 1993-2007 Vols. 1 & 2
   by RD Armstrong (2008)

El Pagano and Other Twisted Tales by RD Armstrong
   (short stories—2008)

New and Selected Poems by John Yamrus (2009)

The Riddle of the Wooden Gun by Todd Moore (2009)

Sea Trails by Pris Campbell (2009)

Down This Crooked Road—Modern Poetry from the
   Road Less Traveled edited by RD Armstrong and
   William Taylor, Jr. (2009)

The Long Way Home edited by RD Armstrong (2009)

Drive By by John Bennett (2010)

Modest Aspirations by Gerald Locklin & Beth Wilson
   (2010)

Steel Valley by Michael Adams (2010)

Hard Landing by Rick Smith (2010)

A Love Letter to Darwin by Jane Crown (2010)

E / OR—Living Amongst the Mangled
   by RD Armstrong (2010)

Ginger, Lily & Sweet Fire—A Romance with Food
   by H. Lamar Thomas (2010)

Whose Cries Are Not Music by Linda Benninghoff
   (2011)

Dog Whistle Politics by Michael Paul (2011)

Made in the USA
Middletown, DE
09 July 2020